Perpetual Innovation™: Innovator's Primer 3.0

The Basics on Intellectual Property Protection for the Creator and Inventor

By

Elmer B. Hall & Robert M. Hinkelman

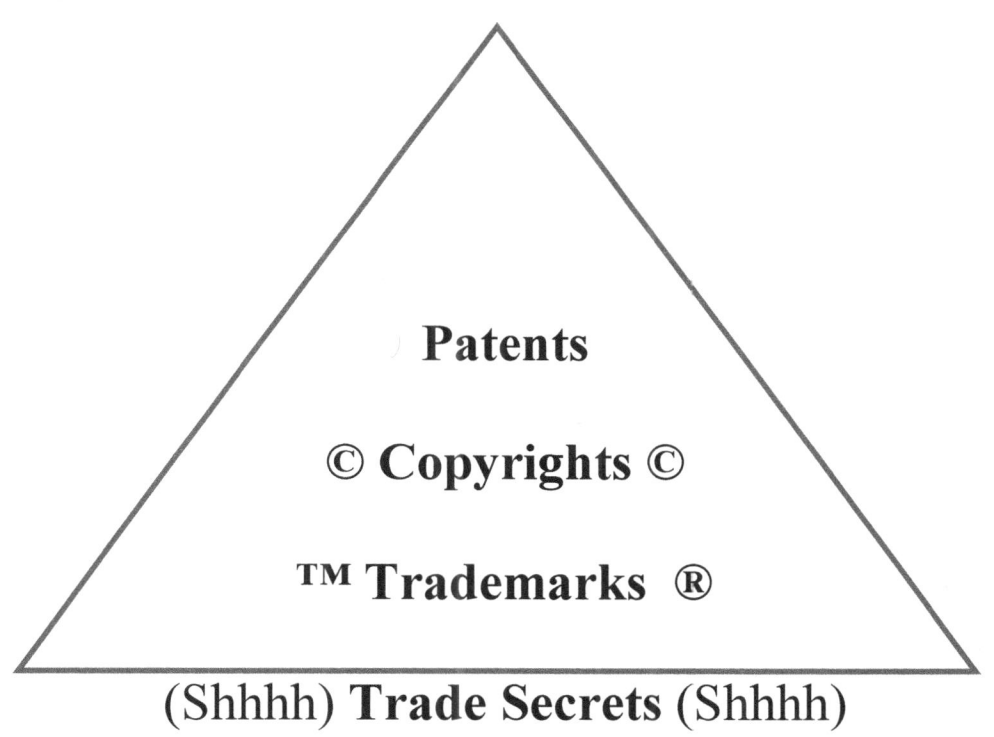

Patents

© Copyrights ©

™ Trademarks ®

(Shhhh) **Trade Secrets** (Shhhh)

> **Perpetual Innovation™**
> **Innovator's Primer 3.O**
> **The Basics on Intellectual Property Protection for the Creator and Inventor**
> by
> **Elmer B. Hall**, DIBA, MBA
> *President,* **Strategic Business Planning Company**
> *Doctoral Facilitator & Dissertation Mentor*
> **University of Phoenix Online**
> and
> **Robert M. Hinkelman**
> *Director of IP Commercialization and Strategic Planning,*
> **Strategic Business Planning Company**

This *Innovator's Primer* is a condensed version of the *Patent Primer 3.0*, which is now a stand-a-lone booklet based on *Appendix B* in the first edition of a guidebook by Elmer Hall and Robert Hinkelman: **Perpetual Innovation™: A Guide to Strategic Planning, Patent Commercialization, and Enduring Competitive Advantage**.
(Look for the 2.0 version of the Patent *Guide* at LuLu Press: **ISBN: 978-1-304-11687-1**)
(Look for the *Patent Primer 3.0* at LuLu Press: **ISBN: 978-1-329-17833-5**)
Visit SBP's LuLu storefront at: www.lulu.com/spotlight/SBPlan
Copyright @ 2007, 2008, 2013, 2015 by Strategic Business Planning Company.
ISBN: 978-1-329-23954-8

Strategic Business Planning Company does strategic consulting including: Strategic Planning Workshops, StratPlans, Business Plans (www.SBPlan.com), Strategic IS Plans (www.SISplans.com), International Feasibility Analysis and Patent Commercialization Planning (www.IPPlan.com). Contact the company at:
> **Strategic Business Planning Company**
> www.SBPlan.com E-mail: ip@IPPlan.com Telephone: (954)704-9100
> 1702 N. Woodland Blvd #116167
> DeLand, FL 32720

No part of this book may be reproduced or transmitted in any form or by any means, electronic or mechanical, including photocopying, or by any information storage and retrieval system without permission in writing from Strategic Business Planning Company, with the exception of short excerpts for book reviews. All rights reserved. This book contains the ideas and opinions of its authors and is designed to provide reliable, competent and accurate information on the subject matters covered. It is sold with the understanding that the authors (and publisher) are not engaged in rendering legal, accounting, financial or other professional services by publishing this book. To address each individual's situation, the appropriate professional should be consulted regarding suggestions made in this book or inferences made from it. The publisher and authors specifically disclaim all responsibility for any risk, loss, or liability incurred directly or indirectly as a consequence of the use or application of the content of this book.

Trademark notices: COMPASS®, *Safe Harbor*™, *Perpetual Innovation*™, and *Plans that every business needs*™ are trademarks of Strategic Business Planning Company. All trademarks and copyrights mentioned in this book are the properties of their respective owners.

Table of Contents

- SBP Consulting & Planning 3
- Perpetual Innovation™: Innovator's Primer 3.0, The Basics on Intellectual Property Protection for the Creator and Inventor 4
  - Introduction 6
  - Overview of Patents First: One of the Great Equalizers of our Time 6
- Types of Intellectual Property (IP) 11
  - Copyrights 12
  - Trademarks 14
  - Trade Secrets 16
  - Standards and Commons 17
- Patents 18
  - What Can Be Patented? 18
  - Types of Patents? 20
  - Disclosure and First-to-File 22
  - Value of IP 24
  - You Missed the IP Boat, Are You Sunk? 27
- Research and Recommendations 29
  - Recommendations 30
- Conclusions 31
- References 33
- Append A: US Patent and Trademark Office Links 34
  - Popular PTO Links 34
  - GOV Resources 34
- About Strategic Business Planning Company (SBP) 35
  - About COMPASS® and Perpetual Innovation™ 35
  - Perpetual Innovation™: Patent Commercialization, and the Patent Primer 3.0 36
  - Sustainability Planning 37
  - Elmer Hall 37
  - Robert "Bob" Hinkelman 37

SBP Consulting & Planning

Strategic Business Planning Company (SBP) helps clients develop *plans that every business needs*™. SBP plans and planning processes focus on flexibility and sustainability. SBP plans including:

- *Business Plan* to plan out an entire business, strategy through implementation.
  IP Business Plan for businesses that that are patent or invention based (see IP Plan).
- *Strategic Plan* (*StratPlan*) is a high-level plans for larger organizations that is followed by detailed division (LOB) plans, as well as, an IP Plan &/or a SISPlan.
- Divisional or Line-of-Business Plans (*LOBPlans*) are business plans for specific markets or divisions of an organization. *Strategic Information Systems Plan* (SISPlan) is a specialized IT division plan that focuses on all aspects of the organization's information technology.
- *Scenario Plan* is a strategic planning tool that is added to the regular planning process to anticipate – and plan for – extraordinary or pending industry events: political, economic or technical.
- *Sustainability Plan* integrates triple-bottom-line (social, environment, and economic) into a plan to meet the requirements of a low carbon economy where social responsibility and carbon footprint are critical metrics plus profitability (real long-term profitability, not artificial measures).
- *Intellectual Property Commercialization Plan* (IP Plan) integrates all aspects of the product pipeline – R&D, patenting, marketing and licensing – to provide a strong and enduring competitive advantage.

ip@IPPlan.com © 954-704-9100 © www.IPPlan.com

Perpetual Innovation™: Innovator's Primer 3.0, The Basics on Intellectual Property Protection for the Creator and Inventor

We at Strategic Business Planning Company love creators and innovators. For many creative people, their minds work differently. But each one of us has a creation inside of us: maybe it's a book or a poem; maybe it's a new way to open and close things. Usually, where one idea balloon pops, there's an eruption of shapes and colors that follow.

And all of us have come up with an invention or two. But many of us don't act on our creative ideas. Probably the two biggest roadblocks to moving creations from dream to market is uncertainty related to mechanics. What to do with the creation, once completed? And, how to protect the innovation? We think that those two roadblocks should be reversed. You probably want to know how to protect your idea first. And then, if you can protect it, go about the best way to move it forward. Without protection, it may be too risky – or too expensive – to swim in shark-infested waters.

We want inventors and creators to have the quickest way to understand the Intellectual Property (IP) options available. We think creators and inventors should be easily and quickly able to evaluate the relevant intellectual property options for them and – equally important – the IP that is not so relevant.

In short, the purpose of this Primer is to quickly put the power of Intellectual Property into the hands of the creators of the ideas and inventions. If there is money to be made from these creations, the creative minds behind the innovations should reap some, if not all, of the benefits.

Note. If you are more of an inventor, you will want the *Patent Primer 3.0* which includes everything from the *Innovator's Primer 3.0*, but more detail about patenting and patent costs.

Perpetual Innovation™
Patent Primer 3.0: Patents, the Great Equalizer of our Time
An Overview of Intellectual Property for Inventors and Entrepreneurs

ISBN: 978-1-329-17833-5

Introduction

Intellectual Property (IP) is critically important. There are few companies, anywhere, that do not have some dependence on IP. Many companies live or die based on their IP. Surprisingly – astoundingly really – many businesses and most business schools do not appreciate how critical IP has become to business success (or failure). This under appreciation of IP is a broken paradigm. An outdated mindset for businesses focused on physical assets that were so important last century like shipping lines and factories, not the intangible assets that support today's value proposition. For most companies, IP forms the basis of *sustainable competitive advantage*.

For the individual creator of art, stories, music, songs, or inventions, intellectual property is critical to your innovation. Without being able to protect your creations and discoveries, it might not be worth the effort to try to market and sell. Simple steps can be taken to protect your creations.

The topics addressed are:
- What is an overview of the various types of IP?
    - Copyright
    - Trademarks
    - Trade Secrets
    - Standards & Common use
    - Patents
- What are some rules-of-thumb or recommendations for IP?
- What conclusions can be drawn about IP in general, and patents specifically?

This primer is useful for all people who create and invent; it is especially important for entrepreneurs, corporate staff and people new to the world of IP. Many graphics have been included to quickly convey key concepts.

Overview of Patents First: One of the Great Equalizers of our Time

During the *Industrial Revolution*, and way back in the day of the *robber barons* (the wealthy owners of mines, ranches, trains, hotels, shipping lines, etc.), the value of the firm – and its assets – where largely physical things. It is easy to plan and build clear accounting practices around physical assets. It is relatively easy to value physical assets. Even way back then, the market value of a business as an ongoing concern was usually more than the firm's *book value* or *net worth* (closing the business, selling off its assets at the exact accounting value and paying all liabilities).

Today, most companies exist – in part or in total – because of their intellectual property (IP). Look at the big pharmaceutical companies where about $300B of annual sales will lose patent protection over 5 years ending in 2018. Blockbusters such as Plavix® and Lipitor® lost protection and Viagra® is in the process of losing U.S. patent protection. The expiration of major patents is aptly referred to as a "patent cliff", the potential massive drop-off in high-priced sales when generics are allowed. The company losing patent protection would then try to switch to follow-on patents and branding to maintain market share and some pricing power. The loss of patent protection to the public domain after enjoying a partial (or full) monopoly is a big adjustment.

IBM has been the king of US patents for decades, having more than 7,000 patents issued in 2014 and the most issued per year since 1992. Apple and Samsung are locked in a global fight on smartphone/smart-pads technology – certainly a fight to the death for anyone else trying to enter this market. Only Microsoft and Google can compete in this war of the big four. Microsoft has armed itself with patents, including a portfolio of $1B from AOL. Google purchased Motorola Mobility for about $12.5B with its smart phone technologies. Blackberry and HP (with its aging patent technologies) are destined for extinction if they cannot figure out a smart way to adapt.

Down at the chip and processor level, there is a similar war. ARM Holdings is a company that invents a lot, but makes nothing. ARM's chips are licensed to dozens of chip makers, and those chips are the heart (and other vital organs) of most smartphones (and the *internet of things*). Broadcom and Qualcomm are in the mix. Intel, the perennial patent holder in PC technology is struggling to keep from losing relevance like Advanced Micro Devices (AMD).

Microsoft might be considered the king of copyright based on software; but Microsoft has amassed a huge patent war chest in addition to its continued copyright protection. Software might also have patent protection in several ways, including patents associated with new hardware, new designs and new business methods.

Disney gains most of its sales and market value based on copyrights: the characters, movies, books and toys are all copyrighted. Trademarks also give leverage to the branded product franchises and theme parks.

<u>International</u>. Since China finally signed on to intellectual property treaties, the Chinese Patent Office has ramped up its level of activity. China was the 5th busiest patent office a few years ago, but in 2012 China's PTO became the world's busiest. Given China's poor history of intellectual property protection, this high volume is very interesting. Companies and inventors need to protect their IP in the largest economies of the world, and China is on a trajectory to surpass the United States' economy (GDP) by 2020.

Patents are filed in the countries based primarily on the size of the economy and the degree to which IP is respected. The top countries have historically been the United States, Japan, Germany, and the UK. Canada, Australia and France might also be included. The larger economies that are frequently skipped are Russia, India, Italy, Spain and Brazil where intellectual property protection is weak.

<u>IP Power</u>. Do not underestimate the power of intellectual property. IP is the strategic competitive advantage that enables many entrepreneurs to successfully launch new companies. IP is the reason that most successful companies exist. IP protection creates and maintains the value of razors (Gillette's 2 blades, 3 blades; Schick's 5 blades & 6 blades), vacuum cleaners (Oreck, Dyson), and virtually everything in infomercials from the ThighMaster® to the Wonder Mop® to Gorilla Glue® to The Bullet®.

There have been millions of patents issued in the United States including bras, dynamite, transistors, integrated circuit, laser and fiber technologies, nanotechnologies and more. One blogger suggested that, historically, the top nine inventions are: cotton gin, electric motor, ice machine, telegraph, phonograph, light bulb, adding machine, airplane, and sliced bread (10 great inventions, 2008). The last of these has joined the vernacular as the common phrase of the best idea or invention "since sliced bread" based on the 1932 US patent No. 1,867,377.

<u>Patents are Powerful and Scalable</u>. Patented technology is scalable. Other companies cannot use your patented technology without your consent; often consent comes in the form of a licensing agreement where they pay royalties for every unit produced and sold. A company using your technology without

permission – infringing on your technology – can be legally required to stop by a court order (enjoined). Willful infringement is subject to treble damages! Wow!

That's right, if profits are $5 the violator will potentially be subject to $15 per unit in damages. As part of an infringement settlement when you sue them, an infringer may be forced to discontinue all sales, or agree to some percentage of future sales – say 5% – in royalties. The patent holder can often make as much in royalties and not actually make anything – thereby avoiding all the costs associated with manufacturing, distribution, sales, and service.

A BIG Infringement Case. Think about one of the largest infringement case in history, the $1B settlement Apple won in the U.S. against Samsung in 2012. Imagine Samsung's relief when the judge in early 2013 decided that Samsung had not "willfully" violated Apple's design patents! A willful violation would leave Samsung with the possibility of treble damages, $3B. Samsung is, of course, appealing the infringement case. The two companies are locked in battle in dozens of courts worldwide. (Expect numerous books on this story and business cases on the strategies.)

In short, a patented technology can result in about 20 years of monopoly market protection. And companies that do not have the technology can be squeezed out of the market or forced to share part (a little or a lot) of the profits with the patent holder.

Being vigilant is important. As competitors eye your high profit margins year after year, they will be motivation to capture some of that profit for themselves. And they will use ethical and even not-so-ethical methods.

IP is Highly Investible and Fundable. A company with patent protection is far more investible than a company without IP. The upside potential on investments in patented technology may be 100% to 1000% return on investment (ROI). Unfortunately, a business concept that is introduced based on public technology can be immediately duplicated; so if the business is successful, the company can immediately expect competition. That likely makes the business concept a bad investment with low or negative ROI.

Inventions with intellectual property protection provide the basis for a successful business venture. IP can often offer massive scalability. Use of the Internet can create scalability as well (eBay, Priceline, and Facebook). Information Technology (IT) – especially the Internet – combined with IP provides double the scalability, growth potential and investment potential. With the Internet, there's also the ability to sell you products to anyone, anywhere in the world. The combination of IP and IT can create the "Wow!" factor that will entice both short- and long-term investors.

Licensing. Speaking of investment potential, having a patent (or even "patent pending") means that, once the patent issues, companies selling your technology must pay you royalties or face the ugly alternative of possible treble damages from infringing. Offering exclusive (or even non-exclusive) licensing can result in huge profits without any effort to manufacture and sell. As well, protection in other countries can provide the option for licensing in those countries without any direct exposure to the risks of the country.

Licensing can take several forms. The most common structure is based on a fixed amount per unit or a royalty as a percentage of sales (or both). A royalty of 1-5% of sales is typical. More than 10% of sales is uncommon. The patent holder will want audits to ensure the accuracy of sales (and royalties). In the immortal words of President Reagan regarding the U.S.S.R.'s nuclear dis-armament, "Trust, but verify."

Cross-licensing agreements are rather common. This is where two companies agree to pool some or all of their patents. Often this where they both agree that "I won't sue you, if you won't sue me." The collective patents may be so formidable; when combined they can effectively form a duopoly, and keep everyone else out of their product market(s).

The CNBC show *The Shark Tank* brings venture capitalists (*sharks*) together with entrepreneurs who are pitching their business ideas for equity investments. It is interesting to watch the sharks go into a feeding frenzy when there is a good business idea that has strong intellectual property. But, they turn with a vengeance on the entrepreneur who is going *naked* – IP-wise – into the big bad world of business. There is a 30-second clip of an episode where all the sharks are in on the investment, until they find out that the patents are *not* part of the investment. Within 5 seconds, all 5 of the sharks are *out*. The two entrepreneurs huddled and figure out a way to put ownership of the patents into the equity deal… With the IP protection back in play, all of the sharks are chummed back into the bidding war, and the feeding frenzy resumes.

Essentially, everyone everywhere should be trying to build IP protection.

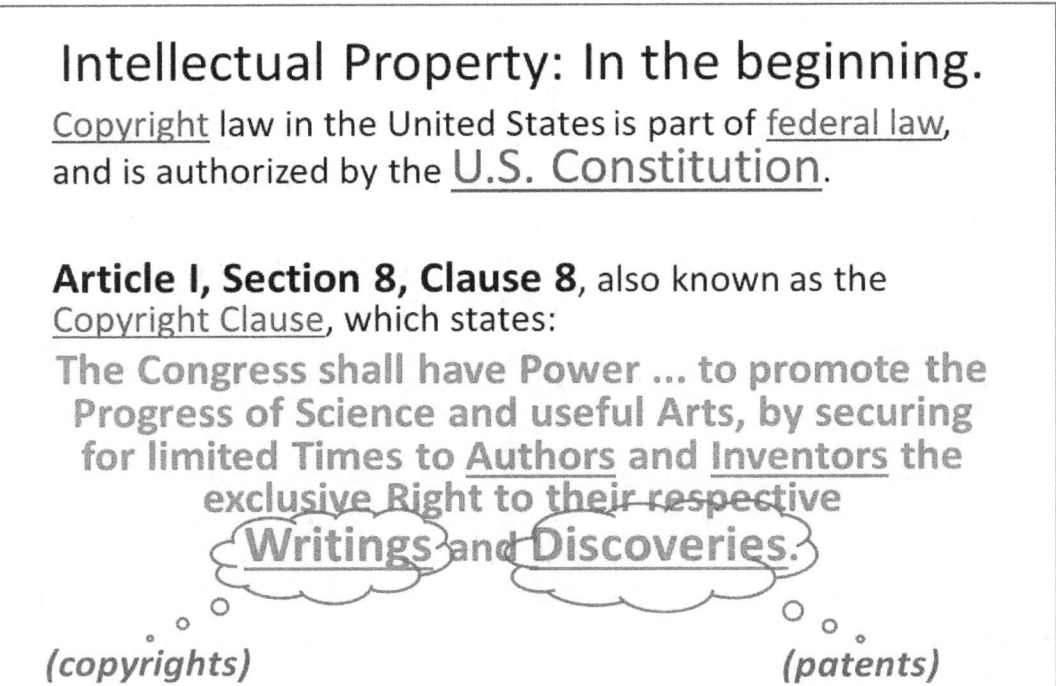

Types of Intellectual Property (IP)

Fortunately, some types of IP are at a very reasonable price. . . Free!

Intellectual Property gets is beginnings in the US from the Constitution. That's right, the Founding Fathers including protection for *creative works* and *discoveries* in the constitution. The Constitution offers protection to writers and inventors that have evolved through law and practice into copyright and patent protection.

Thomas Jefferson, a key drafter of the Constitution, was also a prolific inventor (new plow technologies, for example). "That's right, Thomas Jefferson was not only an inventor of State, he was often in a state of invention; and he was able to elevate IP to a right granted by the constitution, and extended by legislation." (Hall & Hinkelman, 2007, p. 15). Jefferson also set up the U.S. Patent & Trademark Office and become the first director. Ironically, he was not a firm believer in patents and never filed for patents on his own inventions, allowing them instead to enter the public domain and be freely used by everyone. Eventually, however, he did warm to the concept of creativity protection.

An overview of the types of intellectual property protection is needed first before addressing patents in detail. IP tools can be integrated together for the best possible sustainable competitive advantage for the company and each product line. IP can be used by the individual entrepreneur with equal effectiveness. The types of IP are:
- Copyright & Trademarks
- Trade Secrets
- Standards and Common use of Materials and Inventions
- Patents

Intellectual Property (IP)

IP is part of US Federal law and authorized by Constitution.

1. Copyright © for software, books, etc. (free, but...)
   - Individual (death + 70 years... but lots of exception)
   - Corporation for 95 years (125 if not disclosed immediately)

   Lots of Exceptions...

2. Trademarks ™, ℠ for names and slogans. Can last indefinitely (free, but formal registration ® is advised)

3. Trade Secrets (lost to public domain when exposed)

4. Patents: Formal filing at USPTO or global (PCT)
   - Several types: utility, plant, business method, and design
   - Protection of ~20 years. (Design only for 14 years)
   - Fees when issued and at the 3.5, 7.5 & 11.5 years
   - Per country patent; international protection is complicated

Copyrights

"*Copyright* (or author's right) is a legal term used to describe the rights that creators have over their literary and artistic works. Works covered by copyright range from books, music, paintings, sculpture, and films, to computer programs, databases, advertisements, maps, and technical drawings." World Intellectual Property Organization.

> In an unusual departure from normal government processes, getting an original work copyrighted is automatic. When an author creates a work in the United States that meets the criteria for copyrighting, *it is!* The copyright is proclaimed by putting a familiar copyright notice on the document. This notice must have three elements; the word "copyright" or the "©" symbol, the year of the first publication and the name of the copyright holder. (Hall & Hinkelman, 2013, p. 137)

Copyrights for pictures and documents and other "original works" are obtained free when the original works are designated as *copyrighted* original works with the familiar © symbol and/or the word "copyright." The work can be registered with the U.S. Copyright Office for $65 (or as low as $35 electronically). See www.Copyright.gov for copyrighting information and fees. A copyright for an individual lasts for his or her lifetime plus 70 years. For multiple artists/writers this would be 70 years after the last one dies. A corporation's copyright lasts for 95 years (up to 120 years if not disclosed initially). There are many exceptions to copyrights such as non-US citizens.

IP: U.S. <u>Copyrights</u>

Copyrights (life span: Individual's life + 70; or 95 years for corp.)

- Too simple! (downright non-government in concept).
  Written work, music, graphics, architectural designs, sounds, etc.
- Simply use ©, or "Copyright", or "Copr." in all uses of the written materials.
- Register with the Library of Congress (& ISBN # for books) at: www.copyright.gov
- Register with U.S. Customs Service for protection against the importation of infringing copies at www.cbp.gov/xp/cgov/import   *Lots of Exceptions...*
- No "international copyright" but treaties/agreements...
- <u>Person(s)</u>: death + 70 years *
- <u>Corp</u>: 95 years (up to 120, if not disclosed for 25 yrs) *
- A 1998 law extended copyrights by 20 years: "**Mickey Mouse Protection Act**"!☺
  (Also called the Sonny Bono Act.)
- $85 ($35-$55 with e-filing)

Copyright includes the following types/works:
- Literary
- Musical
- Dramatic
- Pantomimes and choreographic works
- Pictorial, graphic, and sculptural works
- Audiovisual works
- Sound recordings
- Derivative works
- Compilations
- Architectural works

Authors, actors, music groups, and most types of entertainment owe their fortunes to copyright. Books, movies, and songs come to mind first related to copyright protection, but software is usually protected by copyright as well. Copyright forms the basis for the huge value that Microsoft has developed in operating systems and software. Now Microsoft augments its copyrights with a large war chest of patents.

A 1998 law – fondly referred to as the *Mickey Mouse Protection Act* – extended copyrights by 20 years; so now Mickey's ears are protected for Disney well into the 21st century. The first Disney cartoon character would have entered the public domain in 2003; now that will not start to expire until 2023.

As with other types of IP, there is no such thing as an *international copyright.* Many countries have similar copyright common law and treaties which provide some assistance in extending the US copyrights to other countries. The publishers and distributors of copyrighted materials (books, articles, etc.) will typically accommodate the best international protection that is reasonable. As an author (creator of books, art, music or software), it is your job to negotiate your royalties on international as well as domestic sales.

Sadly, pirating of copyrighted materials is even more prevalent internationally than domestically. Filing for copyright protection, however, is a critical first step in taking criminal and/or civil action against thieves. That is, ownership of the materials must be established before criminal or civil actions can be pursued. *We offer a special thanks to those ethical readers who have a legal copy of this Primer; many readers are not so honest.*

Trademarks

As with copyrights, basic trademark protection is free! Simply designate a word, phrase or image as trademarked™, or service marked℠, every time you use it. A mark can be formally registered with the PTO. Once a mark has been approved, the *registered trademark*® symbol must be used. Free might be good, however, no marketing manager or advertising consultant will want to invest huge amounts of money on a *brand* for a named product line without a clear and exclusive ownership of the slogans and logos involved; they will insist on filing to register the marks.

Corporate names, Internet domain names and trademarks are a critical part of brand building and need to be carefully coordinated to have the strongest effect. This is called *trade dress*, all dressed up and ready to go to work.

Trademark symbols, words and phrases can be registered with the USPTO. A trademark lasts forever provided it is continuously used (and appropriate maintenance fees are paid for a registered mark). The U.S. trademark does not protect the mark in other countries. (Visit the World Intellectual Property Organization, www.WIPO.int, for information on international trademarks and international patent protection.)

IP: Trademarks™

Trademarks (life span: forever if maintained)
- Can start by simply designated the mark.
- Simply use Trademark symbol™ or Servicemark℠.
- Register with the US PTO for "registered" trademark or service mark. www.USPTO.gov
- No "international" trademark. Need to file in each country/territory.

Must Maintain! Pay renewals or trademark dies! ®

A trademark may be designated by the following symbols:

™ => unregistered trade mark, that is, a mark used to promote or brand goods

℠ => unregistered service mark, that is, a mark used to promote or brand services

® => registered trademark, formally registered w/gov.

Trademarks are a critical part of brand development. Trademarks are especially important as copyright and patent protection expires. Watch, for example, how Intel brands its line of processors as well as each new version. The combination makes even the most novice computer user, look for an Intel® computer with a *Pentium® inside*™. Also, the pharmaceutical companies try to build a very strong *brand name* following so that consumers will be reluctant to buy the *generic* brand once the patent expires. Consumer recognition and loyalty is the holy grail of branding. Think about the place that Kleenex® holds in the facial tissue market?

Trade Secrets

Trade secrets pertain to ideas, formulas, and ingredients that can be kept secret for some period of time. Usually, secrets would apply to internal processes. Search engines (like Google) will keep the internal processing and algorithms of their search engines confidential. The internal processing within a factory might be a trade secret. Work in the lab might be kept secret for some time. But once a produce is introduced for sale, the product and the invention enter the public domain unless measures are taken for other types of intellectual property protection.

> ### IP: Trade Secrets ... Hush! ...Shhhhhh
> (life span: forever... or until no longer secret...)
> - Examples are formulas for Coke-a-Cola and KFC
> - Can be licensed with strong confidentiality/NDA
> - Can't be in a product or service where it can be reverse-engineered.
> - Hard to keep secrets... (leaks, hacks, etc...)
> - "Disclosure" of the invention needs to be in formal patenting process.
> - Patents must be filed before public disclosure. **Shhhhh!** ... or jeopardize patent ... invention "lost" to public domain.
> - Someone else may "invent" the same product.
> - In first-to-file counties – as the US now is – you can be blocked from your own invention if some else gets there first.
>
> What are several famous trade secrets?

Two of the biggest trade secrets of all time are the secret ingredients to Coke a Cola and Kentucky Fried Chicken. (With Coke, the secret ingredient originally was cocaine; but apparently it's not part of the current *secret*.) Thomas' Muffins is a huge trade secret; even though the ingredients are known, the process for getting the fluffy air-pockets within the muffin remains secret.

> It might seem that a good approach would be to hold technology in confidence for a period of time and then patent it once the technology is exposed. Bad idea! If technology is not patented soon after its invention, *it cannot be!* And the right to patent is lost. (See the section on *Disclosure and First-to-File*.)

The need to file a patent "soon after invention," is relative and working to perfect the technology – designing, prototyping, etc. – before filing a patent is reasonable. (The authors sometimes recommend filing a *provisional* patent early and refining the technology for the full patent application within a year.) But just sitting on new technology – holding it as a trade secret, really – has certain problems in terms of patentability. If the technology gets *disclosed* to the public outside of the formal patenting process, it can enter the public domain and the ability to patent it could be lost.

The biggest risk, however, is that someone else may also come up with a similar idea and patent the idea first. (Hall & Hinkelman, 2007, p. 148)

Hall and Hinkelman (2007) advise developing a *Trade Secret Plan*, for anything that will be kept confidential for any length of time.
> For each (group of) trade secret(s) there will be a security plan to isolate and protect the secrecy, IP alternatives to secrecy, potential measures to be taken against people who leak the secrets and contingency plans for if/when those secrets are revealed. (p. 235)

Standards and Commons

IBM had a large family of patents on the PC technology as the personal computer started to evolve. IBM decided to introduce an "open architecture" so that other companies could build components and accessories for the PC. There are many other cases where companies kept rights to patents or copyrights but allowed people to use them for free. Examples of this are freeware, shareware, and works with *creative commons licensing* like Wikipedia content. *Open Office* and *Linux* operating system(s) are based on open source concepts. Typically, you can use *open source* for free, but you cannot set up a business selling it to other people. (Visit www.OpenSource.org.)

Open source is much different from the "free" apps for smartphones which are protected by copyright and possibly have business method patents. Many of the free versions are simply limited versions of the for-pay apps.
With a new computer checking out the "free" applications is always interesting. Many freebees are simply for demonstration purposes or for a

limited trail period. Many of the "free" versions of programs on your new PC are so limited that they are ungraciously referred to as "craplets".

Battery technologies are rapidly being allowed into the public domain. Elan Musk has offered up battery patents from Tesla and his solar businesses. In 2015, Ford and others have followed with their battery patents. They believe that removing the barriers of patents will allow these high powered batteries to more quickly move to economies of scale. Cheap batteries are critical for the electric car industry. Tesla is building *Gigafactory 1* in Nevada to mass manufacture batteries which should reduce the costs of batteries by 30% or more.

A far bigger market for batteries, however, is related to energy management and renewable energy. Cheap power from off-hour energy times can be used to charge battery packs in homes and businesses; then batteries can be used at times of expensive peak grid usage. Batteries are a wonderful addition to renewable energy as well; they proved an effective backup for times when the sun doesn't shine (nights) or the wind doesn't blow.

Patents

Patents are arguably the most important intellectual property protection mechanism of our time! Patents are a critical form of IP and of protecting innovation. Generally, patents form the basis for businesses and successful entrepreneurship. But first, it is important to understand what can be patented and the various types of patents.

What Can Be Patented?

As part of the deal the government offers with patenting, the patent holder is granted a 20-year monopoly on the invention being disclosed in a patent. Almost anything new and novel is patentable. A patentable invention must be novel (in view of *prior art*), non-obvious, and useful. An invention that can only be used for illegal activities is not patentable.

This section addresses patents in more detail. The types of patents are:
- Utility: Mechanical devices such as plows, lasers, turbines, etc. (20-year)
Special types of utility patents are:

- Plant: Genetically Modified Organism (GMO) such as drought and disease-resistant corn
- Business Method: New business methods such as reverse auctions
• Design: Fancy bottles for pouring oil, detergent, etc. (14-years)

> ### IP: U.S. Patents?
> 1. What can be patented? New and novel.
> 2. Government-granted monopoly on the invention for ~20 years!
> 3. Types of Patents: (LIFE SPAN: ~20 years)
>   - Utility Patents
>   - Design Patents (LIFE SPAN: 14 years)
>   - Plant Patents (as in flora such as new plants; GMO)
>   - Business Method Patents
> 4. Maintenance fees go up: 3.5, 7.5, 11.5 yrs from issue
> 5. International Approach: Patent Cooperation Treaty (PCT)
> 6. Provisional Patent. Temporary, place-holder for 1 year.
> 7. Careful or you'll lose it: "disclosure"; US is now first-to-file like most countries.
> 8. Infringers: enjoined! and/or subject to treble damages! $$$
>   ☹ Huge costs for violating someone's IP! ☹ $$$
>
> *Pay maintenance fees, or patent will lapse into public domain.*

A 1980 law suit (Diamond v. Chakrabarty, 447 U.S. 303) ruled an oil-consuming bacteria, classified as a life form that was established to be patentable. The ruling summarized the statutory law related to inventions that are patentable in this way.

> Congress chose very expansive language in the patent statute. . . such that "anything under the sun that is made by man" is patentable subject matter. (35 U.S.C. §101)

Design patents – such as pretty packaging and layout – last for 14 years, but utility patents extend for 20 years. There are a few exceptions, *term adjustments*, which can increase the 20-year period; these are generally applicable to the pharmaceutical industry where patenting, FDA approval, etc., can dramatically reduce the productive life of a patent.

A relatively new variation of the utility patent is the *business method patent* that pertains to new methods of doing business. Amazon with its *one-click* patent and Priceline with its *reverse bid auction* are examples of formidable business method patents.

Types of Patents?

If anything under the sun can be patented, then what types of patents are there, and what are examples of them?

Utility Patents. Most of the patents that people think about are utility patents – like the internal-combustion engine, dynamite, the air bag, and the intermittent windshield wiper. A car commercial might mention the many patents – thousands even – in the newest model. There are a couple specialized versions of utility patents discussed further in this section: plant and business method patents.

Most of the kitchen and home appliances are patent protected in one or more ways. Think about all the super products introduced frequently on the Home Shopping Network: Gorilla Glue®, ThighMaster®, Wonder Mop®, and more. They all made a fortune based on patents. Often they license the technology during later years. Many such inventions have found multiple competitors once their patent expires. Sometimes they lose relevance as the fad fades.

Plant Patents. Plant patent are related to the green stuff. There are several companies that dominate their markets because of patents on biological engineering or genetic modifications. Foods that *do not* have genetically modified organisms (i.e., non-GMO) should be expected in *organic* food. Organic foods should not be associated with new "inventions" and consequently should not typically be candidates for patents.

Most of the seeds planted in the United States are protected by patent. Monsanto is the giant – but not necessarily the Green Giant – of patent-protected plant seeds. Plus, Monsanto can use DNA tests to see if a farmer is illegally using patented strain of seeds, intentionally or unintentionally.

In 2007, Monsanto dominated about 23% of the world seed market (with about $5B in annual sales); DuPont had about 13%. Monsanto has continued to dominate. In law suits with DuPont, Monsanto claimed market share in the United States for its branded corn seed at about 36%; branded soy seed at 29% share; and cotton at 41%. In the anti-trust law suit, DuPont argued that Monsanto's *combined* products *and* licensing was 98% of the U.S. soybean market and 79% of the corn market. Maybe both are correct when licensing is counted.

A separate massive law suit had been growing as well related to DuPont's infringement on Monsanto's plant patents. Both the anti-trust and the patent infringement suits were finalized in March of 2013. In the patent case, the judge ruled against DuPont finding that they had infringed. Apparently having no sense of humor about the misrepresentations purveyed by DuPont, the judge assessed a $1B settlement based on *willful* infringement. Wow, this gigantic settlement is on par with the U.S. win of Apple over Samsung.

Business Method Patents. Probably the most interesting patents available today are *business method* patents, which applies to a unique way of doing business. These business method patents have become more prevalent and extremely powerful including the unique possibilities for doing business over the Internet (e.g., mobile apps and cloud computing). Business method patents include Amazon's one-click patent, Google's bid-per-ad patent, Priceline's reverse bidding process, and eBay's bidding technology.

Design Patents. Another type of patent is the *design* patent. Copyright or trademark are useful for protecting an image or a design, but a really unique design might be patented. A design patent is only for 14 years, not the 20 year for a utility patent, but it has its place in the protection process. Think of the unique bottle designs for Ketchup and laundry detergent. Those are probably protected by design patents (and frequently the design patents are in addition to the utility patents underlying the functionality of the invention). Design patents do not have the maintenance fees that become significant in the later years of a utility patent. The $1B infringement award for Apple against Samsung in the United States was based on design patents related to copying the look and feel of an iPad. Imagine how big might be the settlements for utility patents associated with functionality and performance?!

Provisional Patent application. A provisional patent application is kind of a place-holder for a formal patent application. There is a 1-year time limit for the regular, non-provisional, patent application to be filed. If the full application is not filed within a year, the provisional patent is abandoned (expires). Since the provisional patent by itself will never be reviewed by the PTO, it does not have to be as detailed as a regular patent application. No claims are necessary, for example. During the year refinements can be made, within limits.

The first filing of the provisional patent is the *priority date* if the provisional is converted to the regular patent (non-provisional). You can think of the priority date as the day the clock starts ticking on patent duration. If a single-step process were used (without the use of a provisional application), the full (non-provisional) application would set the *priority date*. (Patents prior to June 8, 1995 were for 17 years from issue, or 20 years from filing, whichever is longer.)

Filing a provisional patent allows the inventor to enjoy "patent pending" status and designate this in sales materials and product packaging. "Patent pending" is very useful in combination with confidentiality agreements for working with manufactures, potential strategic alliance partners, and investors. At the end of the provisional year, abandoning the technology may be smarter than spending more time and money on it.

Disclosure and First-to-File

Disclosure is the process of letting people know about your invention or business method. Selling a novel product to the public is an example of *public disclosure*. The patenting process represents a special type of disclosure to the government in exchange for a 20-year monopoly on the technology. Even though a patent has been filed, it will be some time before the PTO publishes the application to the public, if at all. Consequently, public disclosure will typically be delayed for more than a year unless someone else makes a public disclosure prior to the PTO doing so. Care must be exercised with public disclosures to avoid invalidating the patentability of an invention in the United States *and in other countries*.

Currently, U.S. patents are published after 18 months of first filing, or when ruled on, whichever comes first. Since the review backlog is more than 2 years, this means that it could be 18 months before anyone will be able to fully understand the invention, except for employees and partners with confidential access. This could be a huge advantage. Your competitor, trying to do a work-around for your "rumored" product, cannot make their final product decisions until you introduce a product based on the patent or the USPTO publishes it. (See sidebar *The Secret to Public Disclosure*.)

On March 16, 2013 the United States switched to *first to file*. Previously the US was *first to invent*, and the switch now makes the US consistent with the rest of the world. The old method, *first to invent*, allowed a person who invented something first, to take legal action and prove that he originated the idea prior to the person who filed first. This process is messy, and offers many opportunities to falsify documents and create fictitious inventor notes.

The downside of the *first-to-file* countries is pretty obvious: the first filer gets the patent without regard for who invented it first. Consequently, someone can legally steal an invention simply by rushing to be first to the patent office. This is why secrecy of inventions under development is very important.

Disclosure, when and how the invention becomes known to the public, is a critical component to the patenting process. In general, the first revelation of the invention should be in the formal patenting process. Introducing the product for sale, of course, represents disclosure; but a letter or a conversation with a manufacturer without first obtaining a confidentiality agreement can represent disclosure as well.

Disclosure without *patent pending* status results in two unhappy alternatives. First, someone else might patent the invention. Second, the invention could be disclosed to the public and the invention "lost" to the public domain; the advantage of invention would be lost entirely. Officially, if an invention is disclosed to the public outside of the patenting process, the invention cannot be patented. There is some flexibility on disclosure and the level of flexibility varies by country. In the US, waiting a year from the time that a product containing an invention has been offered for sale (i.e., public disclosure) should move the technology into the public domain and render it unpatentable. But, during that year, someone else could apply for a patent on the technology.

The first disclosure of an invention – such as selling the product – should always be after it has *patent pending* status. Prior to disclosure, have strong *confidentiality agreements* – a Non-Disclosure Agreement (NDA) – in place is critical. You want to have a signed NDA before talking with anyone about your invention.

Value of IP

The value of IP is important to all businesses (brand and trademarks) and mission-crucial to many (patents and copyrights). Many businesses, and most new business concepts, rely heavily on their IP for competitive advantage. The beauty of IP in general – and patents specifically – is the safety, flexibility in commercialization, scalability and fundability.

Safety. Patents, combined with other forms of IP, can produce what Strategic Business Planning Company calls a *Safe Harbor*™ from the competitive storm. Any new product or idea that starts to realize market success – i.e., sales and profits – will attract competitors like ants to a picnic. The first company to market is usually not the successful player in the market, with IP being the notable exceptions. Related to the first-mover-advantage, "it is often said that nobody wants to be first to market, but everybody wants to be first to be second" (Hall & Hinkelman, 2007, pp. 77-80). Being first and being successful is best assured by patent protection. Otherwise the imitators can easily introduce cheaper products and out sell your product. They do not have to expend the money in R&D or in educating the customers about the new product. Additionally, they can introduce inferior products, switching potential consumers to skeptics. IP can provide a level of safety, which is critical to protect the investment necessary in a new product launch.

Patents offer flexibility in ways of commercialization. The obvious way to commercialize the underlying technology is to make and sell the product yourself. If you did this you would probably try to keep everyone else from making a similar product for some time, while you introduced and sold the product with very high profit margins. After a few years, you might license the original technology (collecting a royalty on every sale by partners and reluctant competitors) and introduce a new-and-improved version of the product, hopefully with new and improved patent technology. This is a common way to work the life-cycle of a product. However, it is possible to license to different markets and/or different countries, so you focus on the markets where you want to produce, while still commercializing the technology through licensing into other markets.

Of the several claims in a patent, some of the claims will have multiple applications. That is, when you make the product that you originally designed the invention to cover, say levitation in a toy, there may be many other applications of the same basic technology, say automobiles. So you might make-and-sell your toys while licensing the technology to other markets or industries.

> ## Making It BIG, Based on IP
> 1. <u>Safety</u>. IP can provide a Safe Harbor™ for your company and products to build a business. Other companies must be cautious about infringing (or license from you immediately).
> 2. <u>Flexible</u> with several ways to <u>Commercialize:</u> manufacture/sale, strategic alliances, license, sell patents or sell company.
> 3. <u>Scalability</u>. The patent protected business can license the technology and let the business partner(s) do the heavy work of making, marketing, selling and servicing the product. Different licenses can be restricted to specific markets or specific countries. (Monitor/verify the sales & collect royalties.)
> 4. <u>Investability & Funding.</u> Companies with IP can be infinitely more profitable than business concepts without IP protection. This massive upside potential is attractive to investors.
> 5. Watch CNBS's *Shark Tank* to see how important IP is to funding.
>
> **Strong IP has bigger chances of "making it BIG"!**
> (See Hall/Hinkelman Guide book on IP Commercialization.)

<u>Commercialize</u>. There are many ways to commercialize patents, and often they are not mutually exclusive. You can license the technology to a competitor at the same time that you make it yourself. You make a percentage and/or specific royalty on every unit they sell. Plus, you make profits on everything you sell, as well. Usually this is done where you keep the main brand name and sell it at a higher price; the alliance partner (competitor, really) sells larger volumes at a lower price. Licensing is especially useful for international expansion, provided you have patent protection in that country/region. For example, a good approach might be to let a German company handle all sales and service in Germany through a country-exclusive licensing agreement. There are additional ways to commercialize patent technology. For example, the patents can be sold. Often, the entire company is sold; this provides the buyer with the existing IP along with the entire invention engine of scientists, inventors and entrepreneurs.

Note that selling the patents will be quick and risk free, but that usually would not be the most profitable alternative. The commercialization of technology can be different in different regions and different countries.

Scalability. Often the ability to commercialize patent technology can be amplified. Frequently, one or more of the claims can apply to different products and even to different industries. Patents related to scheduling, for example, might have thousands of applications in dozens of industries. Building a patent fence around the application of that technology in one industry will have ripple effects into the other industries. A concentrated effort is required to watching for potential infringers in different industries and multiple markets. Active vigilance is a *must do*.

People often think of the Internet when they think of scalability. That is, when you build a site that works well for one user, it will work equally well for 100 or 1 million users. Often, patented inventions can be tied to the Internet, possibly in the form of a business method patent. IP combined with the Internet often offers a massive ability to increase the scale of the invention.

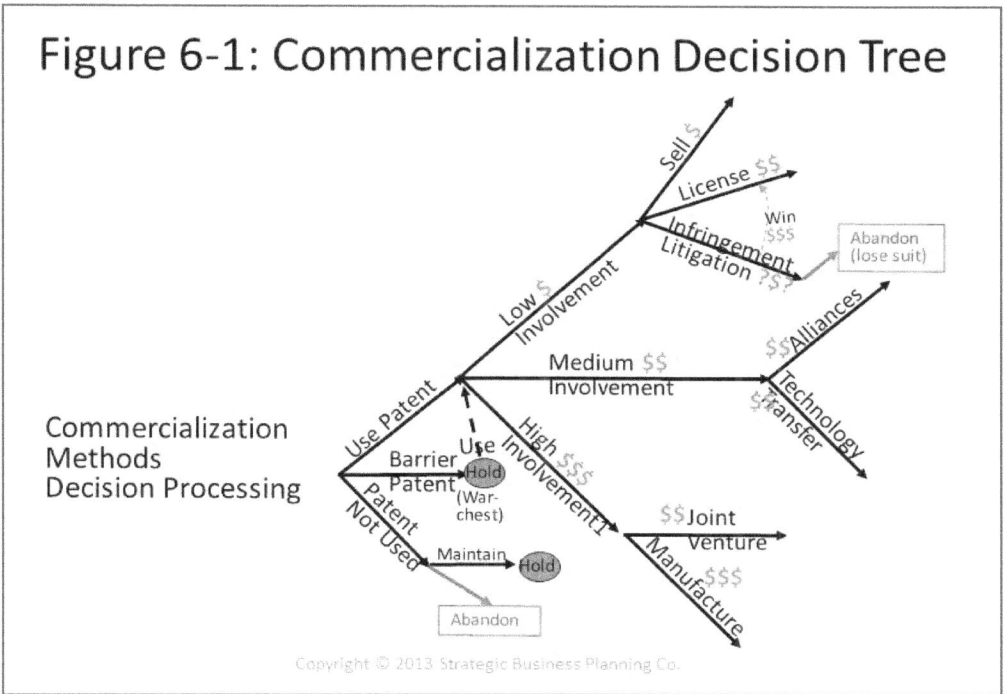

Fundability. Obviously, patents provide the safety, flexibility and scalability that amplify the upside of a business and help to minimize the downside risk. This is exactly what investors seek. An Intellectual Property Business Plan would typically have part of the business designed to manufacture/sell the product and the rest of the business plan designed to accommodate the IP (invention engine and commercialization process). Intellectual property also offers additional investment components. An investor might invest only in the patents, only in the business or some combination of the two. Patents are frequently separated from the initial business that produces the flagship product, possibly into a holding company.

With so much riding on the value of the patents underlying a business, an "opinion" letter from independent professionals might be obtained as to the inherent value of the IP. Professional opinions from patent attorneys and/or business consultants might address such issues as: the chance that the patent will be issued; which claims will likely be accepted and which claims will likely not be accepted; how strong will the patent(s) be if issued; and, what is the nature of the IP landscape that the business is entering? Such analysis can significantly clarify the risks associated with IP and the underlying business ventures associated with IP.

> ### The Ugly, Downside to Patents
> Game Over, if you land firmly on a <u>Patent Land Mine</u>!!!
> 1. <u>Patents can/will kill you</u>, if:
>   - Your business or product lands firmly on someone else's IP!
>   - You find you didn't do *due diligence* on business concept IP.
>   - You did *due diligence* but unpublished patents were in the pipeline.
> 2. <u>Options</u>:
>   - Close your business and cut losses.
>   - Attempt to develop a work-around, apply for patent(s), and implement it.
>   - Negotiate licensing and/or cross-licensing agreements. (Pay royalties.)
>   - Buy the technology (patents) or buy the entire company (with the IP).
> 3. <u>Patent Trolls</u> are companies that camp out on (portfolios of) patents and wait until a company is experiencing product success before attacking. Often the patents are very broad with vague applications. Law suits can cost $1m+; settling can cost $100k-200k. (?Maybe settle, pay, and let the troll go back under the bridge to wait for your competitors?)
> 4. <u>Cyber-squatters</u> take up residence on Internet names (such as previously with Coke.com) in an attempt to extort huge amounts of money, but provide no value-added to the economy.
>
> A business without IP is unarmed in a patent fight!

You Missed the IP Boat, Are You Sunk?

Yes. Sorry!

You need to learn to swim in IP infested waters.

It is a very sad day in the office of a young business when the certified letter shows up officially issuing a "cease and desist" notice related to the core components of the company's flagship product. The official-looking letter might look something like this: "Please contact us immediately to negotiate licensing of this technology. Do not ignore this and continue sales of your product(s). Such sales will be subject to *willful* violation of our patented technology and consequently will be subject to treble damages."

Ouch! This is a very sad day.

The other company with the IP will likely license the technology to you which might represent part, or even all, of your profits. Such cease-and-desist notices to stop production and sales happen far more than you would think. You simply do not hear about all the companies that get shut out of business this way. If your company has IP, then you might have a way to fight back. Otherwise, the options are grim. You might close the business and cut your losses. You might try to develop work-around alternatives that are either public domain or proprietary. A proprietary work around, might be patentable; however, the work-around needs to be a better alternative for you to want to pursue it aggressively.

Vonage and Blackberry landed on patent landmines at the very core of their business technologies. Both were confronted with law suits that threatened to *enjoin* them from doing their core business. Both paid settlement damages. As part of the settlement, both companies agreed to substantial royalties of more than 5% of sales. For a typical company, 5% of sales can easily represent 50% of profits. This was a sad time to be an investor in either company. Vonage had just gone public when it got sued by Verizon for infringing several patents. The final settlement in 2007 had Vonage pay Verizon $58M for past infringement and then pay 5.5% of ongoing customer sales. Ouch! That is expensive for a company that might have only about 5-10% profit margins.

You might be able to license the patent technology from the company you are infringing, maybe with an exclusive license. Additionally, you might be able to license additional technology in the same product area (nascent) to build an arsenal to strengthen your negotiating position. Remember, you do not have to invent technology yourself to use it effectively.

But there is another downside to missing out on the IP technology within your product area. You probably should have identified this technology when you did your *due diligence* on the business idea. This adds a whole new predicament to your responsibility to investors, employees and business partners. Think about all the promises you made and agreements you signed!

The business might not have been launched if careful research would have revealed an obvious patent landmine. Or, it might be that the details of the patent were not visible at the time of the original business plan was development. Careful monitoring of the business product environment (using alerts and readers) should offer a warning the day that an application is published or a patent is issued within your core product areas.

Research and Recommendations

One skill that everyone related to innovation should refine and use relentlessly is related to researching the market and industry. As it pertains to the patents within the industry, the inventor should continually monitor patents being published (even though they have not been ruled on) and patents issued in related fields of invention. IP that conflicts with your own IP should likely be contest as early as possible.

> **Who ya' gonna call to do patent application?**
> - You can do the application yourself... (Lots of issues with this.) (Old adage of the attorney who represents himself...)
> - Registered Agent (may save some money, but not an attorney)
> - Registered Attorney
> - List of registered agents/attorneys: https://oedci.uspto.gov/OEDCI/
> - USPTO wants to talk with only one person (you or the agent)
> - Inventor(s) must be the actual inventor(s) vs. the Agent vs. the Assignee (the formal owner of the patent)
>
> Beware of the invention-help companies!
> (with 800 numbers and such) ⊗ WARNING ⊗

The USPTO (www.USPTO.gov) provides a search engine for issued patents as well as for published, but non-issued, patent applications. The European Patent Office provides a search utility for worldwide patent searches, available at http://ep.espacenet.com. A simpler patent searching engine is available at http://www.google.com/patents/ from Google. Google (and others) offer *readers* that can be programmed to provide alerts when something new happens pertaining to a specific patent, company and/or technology. Trademark information is available from the USPTO as well. International trademarks are available from WIPO (www.WIPO.int). (See USPTO links and resources in the Appendix.)

Find Copyright information at the US Copyright Office (Copyright.gov) or international information at WIPO (www.wipo.int/copyright/en/).

Recommendations

Here are some general recommendations:
1. Use good *confidentiality agreements* and make sure they indicate ownership of joint ideas/inventions. Confidentiality is especially important for investors but should also include consultants and employees.
2. Use those free IP tools of trademark™ and copyright© early and consistently. Then evaluate if additional steps are needed to register the trademarks® or formally file for the copyright.
3. Make sure that names, logos and slogans are not already taken before building a product line around it. It can get ugly (and expensive) if you tromp on someone else's IP.
4. Get to *patent pending* as soon as prudent. This might utilize a provisional patent for a US-targeted invention, or the utilization of a PCT application for an international invention.
5. Use the time in *patent pending* and *international patent pending* status well and wisely in order to position for the best strength and flexibility for the commercialization of the technology.
6. Do not forget to pay the maintenance fees (starting at 3.5 years from issue for patents). But, make sure that you allocate some time prior to the maintenance due dates to reevaluate your technology and be sure that you have time to sell, license or abandon the technology.
7. Remember that we all have strengths and weaknesses. In most cases, selectively employing a knowledgeable professional to work with you to help develop the invention is more cost effective than trying to develop it and registering by yourself.
8. Reevaluate the combined business and patent environment at each stage of bringing the invention to markets. Always think about positioning the technology and product: what is the best single thing that can be done next in order to strengthen the product and the business case for its success. Plan for the patent and product development process to take longer and cost more than projected.
9. Develop an *IP Business Plan* that shows the full picture for commercial success of the technology. This helps you think through the productization and marketing of the final product(s) based on the technology. Revise the business plan to make it more accurate when you have better information, and make it more robust when you need it for planning or investment funding.

10. Don't let infringement or pirating go uncontested, but litigate very cautiously. Remember that they are subject to treble damages if they *willfully* infringe on your patented technologies (after they have been formally notified of the infringement). Exercise *due diligence* as part of your efforts to develop new technology and products.
11. Don't be snookered by the many less-than-reputable "invention help" services, even if they have fancy ads and 800 numbers!
12. Don't force it. Aim for the best positioning of the business/product. Move on to the next invention if you hit a brick wall, but be ready to revive an invention if circumstances change or an opportunity arises.
13. Aim for a family of products (or inventions) not a solitary one. Always have enhancement product ideas on the drawing board. You are an inventor after all, and that passion for the next improvement or the next great breakthrough is what will attract people to you.
14. Augment utility patent protection with other types of IP: design patents, trademarks, and/or copyrights.
15. You don't have to invent IP to utilize it; you might license – maybe license exclusively – technology from other companies.
16. Aggressively and continually look for strategic alliance partners; your technology will usually have multiple applications in multiple industries.
17. Think long-term and sustainably. An invention or product should be renewable, recyclable, etc. If what you do and what you invent is not sustainable, then you already know what the 2.0 or 3.0 version of the product must achieve, don't you?

Conclusions

This primer focuses on providing a quick and efficient overview of the tools of Intellectual Property, and ways to utilize IP for a *sustainable competitive advantage*. IP is always a valuable asset to have on your side, sometimes invaluable. You want to go boldly into business where you are well protected, IP-wise. You definitely do not want to go blindly into new markets where you have not carefully assessed the terrain for IP land mines.

IP is unbelievably important. And it is surprisingly overlooked. There are many reasons why, but it is important that you have started discovering the secret; you are becoming better armed to exist in a competitive world, a world that has become hypercompetitive due to IP and rapid information flow.

There are two things going for the small inventor/creator – three things, really, if the inventor has great ideas. The two great equalizers of modern time are:
1) *Intellectual Property* rights. Patents and copyrights are obviously appreciated for you the creator/innovator/inventor to be reading this. The patent protection should be advanced in lockstep with business decisions. This can provide the best possible positioning so that you are able to leap when opportunities present themselves (or to jump ship if they don't).
2) The *Internet* provides the ability for an entrepreneur to sell a product to anyone, anywhere. This potentially allows the inventor to educate, advertise and sell products very inexpensively. There are virtual marketplaces for products. There are marketplaces for crowdfunding. Even the patents can be licensed or auctioned online. Internet tools can provide metrics, feedback, profit feasibility and proof of concept. If online sales are very successful, it could fund the growth of an empire.

Many people will argue that *education* is a third great equalizer of modern time. Hopefully this Primer has been helpful in this respect as well.

The mix of innovation, education and knowledge is a powerful addition to create equality among innovators and inventors. By you reading this, you are arming yourself to compete in a world of business that can be ruthless, a competitive world where great ideas can and will be copied – especially, when they are demonstrated to be commercially valuable.

You are working with IP, one of the great equalizing toolkits of our time. With the possibility of 20 years of patent protection ahead or 90+ years of copyright protection, it may very well be worth the effort. Bringing to market good solutions to common problems is rewarding all by itself. . . Bringing a creation to the world is rewarding as well… But making a little money – or even a gigantic amount of money – would be nice too.
    Good inventing and creating
    Good intellectual property protection.
    And, good luck!

References

10 really great American patents. (2008, March 31). [Blog by stevenh at Listverse]. Retrieved from: http://listverse.com/2008/03/31/10-really-great-american-patents/

Hall, E. (2009). Strategic planning in times of extreme uncertainty. In C. A. Lentz (Ed.), *The Refractive Thinker: Vol. 1. An anthology of higher learning* (pp. 41-58). Las Vegas, NV: The Refractive Thinker® Press.

Hall, E. (2010). Innovation out of turbulence: Scenario and survival plans that utilizes groups and the wisdom of crowds. In C. A. Lentz (Ed.), *The Refractive Thinker: Vol. 5. Strategy in innovation* (pp. 41-58). Las Vegas, NV: The Refractive Thinker® Press.

Hall, E. (2010). Lessons of recessions: Sustainability education and jobs may be the answer. *Journal of Sustainability and Green Management*. Jacksonville, FL: Academic and Business Research Institute. Retrieved from: http://www.aabri.com/OC2010Manuscripts/OC10079.pdf

Hall, E. B. & Hinkelman, R. M. (2007). *Perpetual Innovation™: A guide to strategic planning, patent commercialization and enduring competitive advantage*. Morrisville, NC: LuLu Press. (Available at the LuLu Press Store for SBP at: http://www.lulu.com/spotlight/SBPlan.)

Hall, E. B. & Hinkelman, R. M. (2013). *Perpetual Innovation™: A guide to strategic planning, patent commercialization and enduring competitive advantage, Version 2.0*. Morrisville, NC: LuLu Press. (Available at: http://www.lulu.com/spotlight/SBPlan.)

Hall, E. B. (2007). *Strategic economic development & marketing plan for Highlands County*. Morrisville, NC: LuLu Press.

Hall, E., & Knab, E.F. (2012, July). Social irresponsibility provides opportunity for the win-win-win of Sustainable Leadership. In C. A. Lentz (Ed.), *The Refractive Thinker: Vol. 7. Social responsibility* (pp. 197-220). Las Vegas, NV: The Refractive Thinker® Press.

Hall, E., Taylor, S., Zapalski, C., & Hall, T. (2009). Sustainability in education: Green in the facilities, but not in the classrooms. Proceedings of the *Society for Advancement of Management*, USA.

US Patent & Trademark Office [USPTO]. (n.d.) United States Patent and Trademark Office, a division of the Department of Commerce. Retrieved May 1, 2015, from: http://www.uspto.gov/

US Patent & Trademark Office [USPTO]. (2015, April 1). *USPTO Fee Schedule, Effective date January 1, 2014*. Retrieved May 1, 2015, from: http://www.uspto.gov/learning-and-resources/fees-and-payment/uspto-fee-schedule

Append A: US Patent and Trademark Office Links

UNITED STATES PATENT AND TRADEMARK OFFICE
http://www.uspto.gov/

See links at: www.IPplan.com/links/

Popular PTO Links
Patent Search   (http://www.uspto.gov/patents/process/search/index.jsp)
Patents: File Online [EFS-Web]
Patents: Check Application Status [PAIR]
Patents Online Services
Patents Term Calculator   (http://www.uspto.gov/patents/law/patent_term_calculator.jsp)
Patents Ombudsman   (http://www.uspto.gov/patents/ebc/)
Trademark Search [TESS]   (http://www.uspto.gov/trademarks/)
Trademarks: File Online [TEAS] (http://www.uspto.gov/trademarks/teas)
Trademarks: Check Status/Documents [TSDR]
Trademark Basics
Official Gazette for Trademarks
Manuals (incl. MPEP and TMEP)
Registered Patent Agents/Attorneys   (https://oedci.uspto.gov/OEDCI/)
Forms & Fees   (http://www.uspto.gov/curr_fees)
World Intellectual Property Organization (http://www.wipo.int/)

GOV Resources
BusinessUSA Start, grow and do business in the USA
SelectUSA The USA is the place for business
FDSys.gov Browse the Federal Register

Copyright Office: www.copyright.gov
        (Library of Congress & ISBN # for books)
Register with **U.S. Customs Service** for protection against the importation of infringing copies at www.cbp.gov/xp/cgov/import
World Intellectual Property Organization (http://www.wipo.int/copyright/en/)

SOURCE: US Patent & Trademark Office (2013). *United States Patent and Trademark Office, a division of the Department of Commerce.* Retrieved on February 17, 2013, from: http://www.uspto.gov/

About Strategic Business Planning Company (SBP)

Common to virtually all of the clients of Strategic Business Planning Company (www.SBPlan.com) is that they have had a new and innovative concept that they wanted to launch in the form of a new business or a new line of business. Occasionally there has been "another" retail store of service business, but often even those businesses had a novel twist, e.g., the old way of doing things but with Internet or application server advancements. Even if the client did not already have intellectual property protection, it was a vital part of the strategic planning process to assure that they had (at least planned for) patenting, copyrights, branding (company name, Internet domain names, trademarks, etc.) during the development of a business plan. In fact, if patent protection were an integral part of the business plan, the entire business plan had to be reorganized to accommodate the multiple possible methods of commercializing the technology both in the product/service produced and in technology transfer (licensing) to other market segments. This Intellectual Property Business Plan (or IP Business Plan) becomes the framework for valuing patent-based technologies where at least one market was serviced by the company directly and other segments were licensed out, thus demonstrating the effort to bring the productized technology to market while presenting the case for potential profitability from all likely commercialization methods.

As it became increasing evident that there exists a huge void in the business planning and valuation aspects of patent commercialization, SBP chose to focus on this unserved, but critically important, market. The consulting process established for a startup company or line of business is like the Patent Business Plan that quickly works through all aspects of the business and documents it. However, for larger firms, SBP has created a consulting process: Commercialization of Patent Assets or COMPASS®. Although COMPASS® applies only to a specific company, there are many generalizations associated with it that apply to all high-tech organizations. That process was developed into a how-to book that is unique in its focuses on the business perspective of patent commercialization – the sustainable, longer-term, competitive advantage that can be gained from IP. Thus the book **Perpetual Innovation™, A Guide to Strategic Planning, Patent Commercialization and Enduring Competitive Advantage** was born. Appendix B in the first edition was actually the original Patent Primer.

About COMPASS® and Perpetual Innovation™

Perpetual Innovation™ describes the strategic planning process necessary for managers and inventors to bringing protected technologies to market. The Hall-Hinkelman book outlines the ways to organize for innovation and how best to commercialize intellectual property (patents) nationally and internationally. Valuation and decision-making methods are presented for assessing the value of technology at early stages and preparing for the best methods of value realization. Key to market success is being first to market, with a superior product and the best possible intellectual property protection. This book focuses on the business side of patent commercialization, those decisions that involve everyone in the organization, not just the patent attorneys and the scientists. Publications of the company are at Amazon and at LuLu press. Commercialization of patent assets, COMPASS®, is a registered service mark for the company and the COMPASS® process is used by SPC to consult with companies on patent commercialization. Perpetual Innovation™ is the name associated with the series of innovation books.

The Outline of Perpetual Innovation

INTRODUCTION: Assessing the Current IP Situation

The PLANNING YEAR:
- Chapter 1: Integrated Planning Year
- Chapter 2: Integrated IP Planning Year

IP Commercialization:
- Chapter 3: Optimizing the IP Process
- Chapter 4: IP Enhancement Strategies
- Chapter 5: IP Valuation/Prioritization

Special Topics:
- Chapter 6: Licensing Strategies
- Chapter 7: IT in an IP World
- Chapter 8: Scenario Planning

IP Management and Decision-Making:
- Chapter 9: Organized for Innovation
- Chapter 10: IP Portfolio Management
- Chapter 11: IP Commercialization Plan

Chapter 12: Conclusion and Measuring IP Progress

Copyright © 2007 Strategic Business Planning Co.

(IP Assessment/Audit → IP Progress Review)

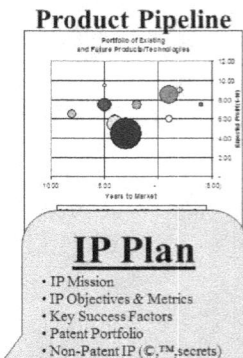

IP Plan
- IP Mission
- IP Objectives & Metrics
- Key Success Factors
- Patent Portfolio
- Non-Patent IP (©,™,secrets)
- Supporting Plans/Documents
- Finalized Budget
- Appendixes

Perpetual Innovation™: Patent Commercialization, and the Patent Primer 3.0

Books and articles on Intellectual Property (IP) are too detailed or to general to be useful for the typical creator, inventor or entrepreneur. Innovators first need a general idea of how and when to utilize intellectual property protection (copyright, trademarks, patents and trade secrets) and how best to utilize these great equalizing tools. The details of IP can be complicated, especially without a clear idea of where to focus. Books on patents tend to avoid specifics on fees and other cost estimates of getting a patent. One reason, of course, is because the fees change, resulting in misinformation. Additionally, there are several different paths for patent protection. People are directed to the US Patent and Trademark Office (www.USPTO.gov) for current processes and fees. The multiple pages of fees and options are confusing. The available information does not help the typical person trying to understand and utilize IP. A simple primer is needed.

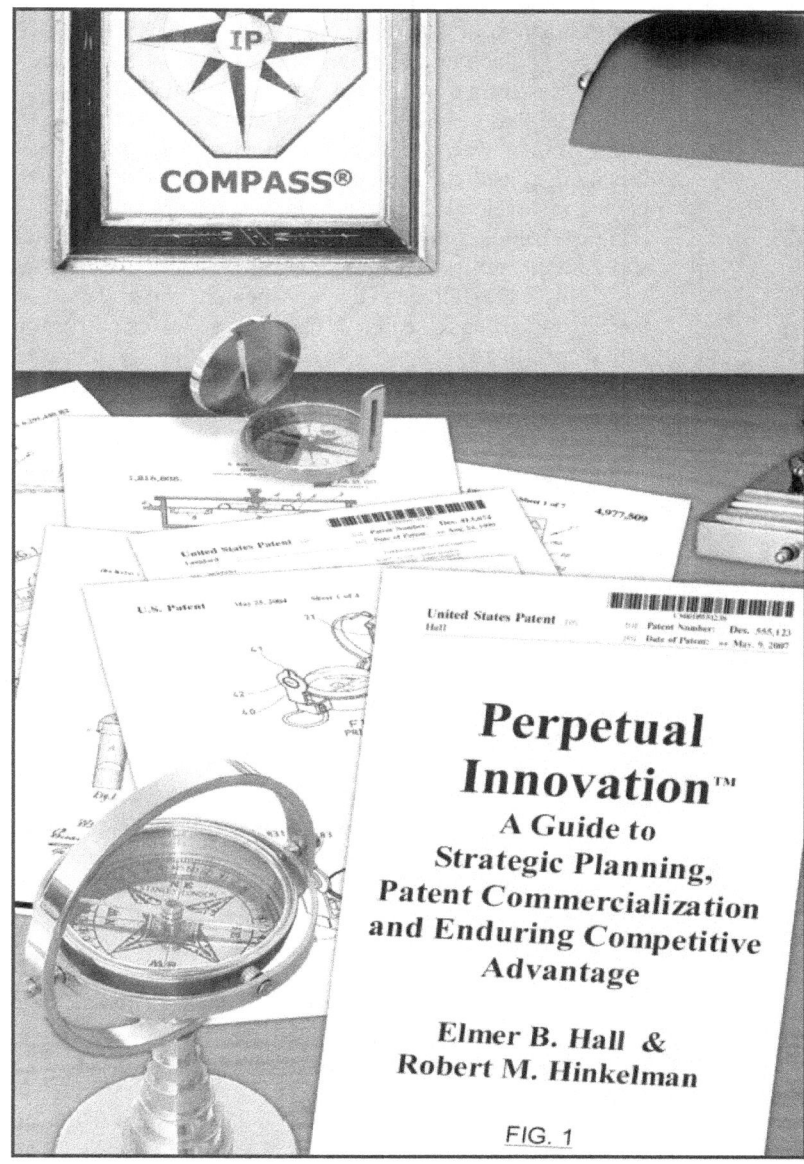

In 2007, Hall and Hinkelman wrote **Perpetual Innovation™: A Guide to Strategic Planning, Patent Commercialization and Enduring Competitive Advantage** for companies to create the best environment for innovation. The *Guide* creates a sound planning process with the best use of patent protection to gain a sustainable competitive advantage. Inventors and small companies can learn much from the book, but it will be most valuable to organizations of a hundred employees or larger which have many products – and patents – to manage. The Guide did not originally describe the basics of patents and patent filing, so we added a basic *Patent Primer* (1.0 version) as *Appendix B* to the book. The patent laws changed dramatically in 2012 and fees increased. Look for the new versions of the *Guide*. The *Patent Primer* is now a stand-a-lone booklet. This new version substantially expands and updates the original.

Sustainability Planning

SBP has moved into *sustainability* planning/consulting. Eventually we all – individuals, businesses and governments – must exercise sustainable practices. Innovation and invention can help with the issues of the environment and non-sustainable business practices. Many of the planning concepts outlined in the COMPASS® process for IP are required in order to conduct sustainability planning. Everyone in the organization must be engaged, for example. It needs to be sponsored at the highest levels of the organization. The importance of it needs to be reflected in the organizations mission, vision and goals. As with IP, sustainability should be integrated into the strategic planning process. A business does not have a real business plan if it does not include a plan to be sustainable. Many of the company's current projects and efforts are related to sustainability, especially energy efficiency (EE) and telecommuting.

Elmer Hall

Elmer Hall has a Doctorate of International Business Administration from Nova Southeastern University as well as an MBA and BA from the University of South Florida. Throughout his schooling, he was a management and research assistant involved in business/trade research and systems development. He taught business at the undergraduate and graduate levels (MBA and MIS) at several Florida universities. He also is a Facilitator and Dissertation Mentor for the University of Phoenix. His "real" education, however, is from his personal entrepreneurial ventures and those of his clients.

Hall has been involved in strategic planning or systems development for hundreds of companies. Many of them were small ventures that he helped develop startup business plans; others were longer-term including consulting activities with IBM, Florida Power & Light and Burger King (Diageo). At FPL he helped to develop the Quality Improvement Program tools that were used throughout the organization to win the *Deming Award for Excellence*. At Burger King he helped develop Y2K worldwide risk assessments, mitigation strategies and business partner contingency plans.

In 1982, Hall created a management and systems consulting company that expanded in 1987 to become Adaptive Research & Design Co., which still continues to operate (and additionally does Data Recovery). In 1995, he took the Business Plan Development line of business and created Strategic Business Planning Company (SBP). He is President and CEO.

Hall has authored and edited hundreds of business plans including IP and IT mission-critical plans. He has been publishing peer-review articles on innovation, sustainability and planning. See several of his publications in the award-winning Refractive Thinker® book series.

Robert "Bob" Hinkelman

Bob Hinkelman has always been inventive and a learning enthusiast. He received a BA in History from Lafayette College before going to AT&T. In over 34 years at AT&T, he held positions in sales, field Operations, Headquarters Network Engineering and Engineering Planning. He played a key role in upgrading the long distance network and its Service Nodes to digital technology and was deeply involved in the 1984 Divestiture of the Bell Companies. After the Divestiture, he moved to the Fortune 500 Business Markets Division where his responsibilities included market research, new service creation, ISDN service development and the prototype of virtual private broadband services. Then, he developed a Business Unit Intellectual Property management process for the Business Services Group including AT&T's first "Pay for Patents" program which became an AT&T standard. In 1995, he moved to the Intellectual Property Division (IPD) where he was responsible for establishing a market focused for business planning, new revenues and core process reengineering. The 1996 Trivestiture created Lucent Technologies; he transferred to Lucent with IPD and most of Bell Labs where he was aggressively involved in the processes of moving IP decision making from labs and law departments into Business Units.

Hinkelman is the Vice President of Strategic Planning & Intellectual Property Commercialization for SBP. He has been actively involved in the strategic planning of clients' marketing and business plans where patented technologies were mission critical. An IP Business Plan approach was created to accommodate the elevation of patent commercialization to the highest strategic levels of planning. He was instrumental in developing the Commercialization of Patent Assets (**IP COMPASS®**) methodology for patent commercialization.

Tech companies need to move to a business-focused, IP-centric structure as summarized in Hall and Hinkelman's book on patent commercialization. Companies applying COMPASS® can expect to be *perpetually innovative* with an *enduring competitive advantage.*

As an aside, look for *prior art* by Hinkelman – mainly landscapes in acrylics – in fine art galleries.

www.ingramcontent.com/pod-product-compliance
Lightning Source LLC
Chambersburg PA
CBHW080855170526
45158CB00009B/2742